PASSION FOR PRESENCE

FINDING THE KEY TO GOD'S HEART

by
Louis F. Kayatin

PUBLISHING · INC

Tulsa, Oklahoma

Passion for Presence
(Finding the Key to God's Heart)
ISBN 0-9657706-2-1
Copyright © 1997 by
Louis F. Kayatin
4125 Leavitt Road
Lorain, Ohio 44053-2300

Phos Publishing, Inc.
P. O. Box 690447
Tulsa, Oklahoma 74169-0447

Dedication

I would like to dedicate this work in honor of my four children: Mary, April, Rebecca and Louis, for it is in their interest and in their generation that I record the *keys for coming into God's presence.*

Nearly every move of God has diminished in intensity by the fourth generation. Today we must not only recover the message of Pentecost, but we are challenged to keep the flame burning brightly until Jesus comes again!

Contents

Foreword by Rod Parsley
Introduction

KEYS FOR COMING INTO GOD'S PRESENCE

About the Author

Foreword by Rod Parsley

In 1993 I met Louis Kayatin — a man of character, conviction and compassion for lost and hurting people. It was during this divine appointment that he said to me, "We are as the minutemen of the Revolutionary War, ready to serve at a moment's notice."

I was honored by such an outpouring of love from Louis and his congregation, the great Church on the North Coast in Lorain, Ohio. Since that time it has been my privilege to know and to work with Pastor Kayatin.

He is a man anointed by God who is full of faith and vision to proclaim the Gospel message with heartfelt passion and to raise the standard to this final generation. His life exemplifies moral integrity, physical purity and spiritual intensity — qualities which are quickly becoming relics of the past.

I believe one of his most distinguishing characteristics, though, is his servant's heart. Pastor Kayatin and his wife, Tina, have ministered to me, Joni and our family personally, as well as to our church, in such a meaningful way. We are both humbled and grateful to him for the wonderful blessing he has been to our lives and ministry.

My pastor, Dr. Lester Sumrall, once told me if you have two or three real friends during your life, you are truly a rich man. Not only is Louis Kayatin a great pastor, teacher and author...he is a dear and faithful friend.

I believe as you read this book, you will discover the mark of true greatness by someone who has paid the price to receive it...and you will know the secret of walking in a **Passion for** [His] **Presence.**

Introduction

There is an ever-increasing curiosity concerning the "acts" of God. People will drive thousands of miles to see some manifestation of God's mighty hand. It seems as though we are looking for some validation for our faith, some confirmation that we are really serving a tangible God. Jesus said in Matthew 16:4 that it is a wicked and perverse or adulterous generation who seeks a sign. Believers today seem to concentrate more on seeking God's hand, (what He can do), rather than seeking His face.

God made His *acts* known to the children of Israel, but He made His *ways* known to Moses (Psalm 103.7). As proven time and time again, the revelation of God's acts did not strengthen the Israelites in their faith. They were quick to murmur, complain and fall away each time God simply did not manifest Himself according to their timetable. When they became restless they would take matters into their own hands.

The acts of God reveal His power.

The ways of God reveal His person.

David asked in Psalm 15:1 NKJV, "Lord, who may abide in Your tabernacle? Who may dwell in Your holy hill?" The Holy Spirit then answered David with three strokes of a brush, painting a picture of one who lives life *abiding* in God.

One who lives continually as a houseguest of God first "walks uprightly" (v. 2). It is he whose inner conduct dominates his outward life (Luke 1:6). The next stroke reveals the color of one who "works righteousness" (v. 2). Systematically and habitually he will align his actions or his outward conduct to harmonize with his inner man (his spirit). Thirdly, the final stroke of the brush reveals one who "speaks the truth in his heart." This requires total honesty, first with one's self, then with God, before man can be completely honest in outward dealings.

The key then seems to be a triangular shaped instrument of three equal sides — walk, work and speak. Each part relies on the other two. For those carrying the complete key, access to God's presence is granted.

Satan has no fear of our knowing the location of God's house (His presence). He does tremble however when, with key in hand, we enter into God's dwelling.

The remaining verses of Psalm 15 provide the shading and highlights to the portrait of one who gains access to the presence of God, dwells in His Holy hill and has His fullness dwelling in them.

As you read you will learn the practical steps to knowing God's ways, which in turn will produce the acts of God, for your personal life as well as for the lives of those with whom you come in contact.

Lord, who shall abide in thy tabernacle?
who shall dwell in thy holy hill?
He that walketh uprightly, and worketh
righteousness, and speaketh truth in his heart.
He that backbiteth not with his tongue,
nor doeth evil to his neighbour, nor taketh
up a reproach against his neighbour.

In whose eyes a vile person is contemned;
but he honoureth them that fear the Lord.
He that sweareth to his own hurt, and
    changeth not.
He that putteth not out his money to usury,
nor taketh reward against the innocent. He
that doeth these things shall never be moved.

Psalm 15:1-5

KEY 1

CAREFUL

1
C A R E F U L

He that backbiteth not with his tongue, nor
doeth evil to his neighbour, nor taketh up a reproach
against his neighbour.

Psalm 15:3

In the very first stage of entering God's presence, the Golden Rule is reinforced by David. It is often the most simple truths that trip us up. We are looking for some deep theological revelation when the answer is right in front of our face.

David perhaps had recognized how doing evil against his neighbor had separated him from God's presence. This "man after God's own heart" allowed himself to be drawn away from his abiding place in God, by the lusts of his own flesh. David dishonored Bathsheba by the sheer force of his personal power. David also dishonored his neighbor Uriah the Hittite by taking that man's wife into his own bed.

The very power David used had been a gift from God — an act of God birthed as a result of David constantly abiding in God's presence. As David walked with God and worshiped Him, God had moved in his behalf, anointing him and setting him in a high place of leadership.

David now found out the loneliness of being separated from God when he put his power to personal, selfish and lustful use. David's anointing for leadership was given to govern the people. A great responsibility comes with any gift.

Today it is not unusual to see a 16-year-old who has been given a new car for their beginning driving experiences. The car is given in love, sometimes with great sacrifice by the parents. It is meant to be used in a responsible manner, such as driving to school and church events and perhaps to a part-time job. It will take some of the responsibility from the shoulders of "mom's taxi service."

It is a gift. It comes from the hearts of those in whose home the teenager has lived. It is birthed from that love relationship and the heart of parents wanting to give good and perfect gifts. With that gift comes new and sometimes overwhelming responsibilities.

The gift must be maintained. Now the teenager must maintain the gift, cherish it and use it responsibly. Suddenly reality sets in as the teen realizes there is a **price** tag. Usually keeping the vehicle clean is not a problem since they are always wanting to show off their gift. It will always look great on the outside, but what about the inside? Oil changes, fluid checks and constant filling station visits are required for the new owner who soon learns the high cost of maintenance. For those who do not learn that lesson, they soon find their gift unusable — burned out, dried out, broken down.

Some only want to use their gift to draw attention to themselves. They develop a great sense of pride in having such a great possession. Blaring music, revved engines and reckless driving result. One careless moment can destroy the gift and the owner and often even other innocent lives.

One reckless act on David's part did just that. God had trusted David with the responsibility for an entire nation, and he laid it on the line for a single irresponsible night. He exchanged the future of tomorrows in a single day.

Ordinarily, David had been careful for those in his charge. When he was responsible for his father's sheep, he fought fearlessly in their defense. He risked his own life for the flock while protecting them against a lion and a bear.

Even before his kingship, he stood bravely in defense of his people before Goliath. He rose above ridicule, refused armor not his own and rescued a nation. He cared more for the freedom of the people than for his own life.

When he had the opportunity to retaliate by killing the man who was jealous of his anointing, who had threatened his life and attacked his good name, he did not. David left Saul in God's hands for judgment. He was careful to do no evil to King Saul.

Am I My Brother's Keeper?

When God confronted Cain regarding the whereabouts of Abel, this was his reply, "Am I my brother's keeper?" (Genesis 4:9). The obvious answer was a resounding YES, but Cain had already missed the point. Having his own way in regard to his offering caused him to lose all sense of responsibility to God and to man (Genesis 4:8).

Moses was careful to do no evil in return for their weaknesses when the Israelites wearied God with their attitude. When God threatened their destruction Moses laid his eternal life on the line for their protection (Genesis 32:11-14).

Abigail ran after David to apologize for her rude husband. Though it was not proper etiquette of the day, she cared more for the lives of her family than for her own reputation (1 Samuel 25:23-31).

Abraham gave up the best of his land to his nephew to maintain peace in his family (Genesis 13:9-11).

Esther was willing to perish if that was what it would take to save her people (Esther 4:16).

Throughout the Old Testament, we see the results of decisions made by those abiding in relationship with God. The firstfruit of abiding is the careful response toward our neighbor.

The New Testament reveals to us the ultimate example of caring in the life of Jesus Christ. He offered Himself up as the final sacrifice to secure our salvation. He paid the price with His life.

When Jesus spoke to the people of His day regarding these responsibilities, He had not yet died. When we read those words today we know the price that was paid and our responsibilities pale in comparison to His death on the cross.

A Stumbling Block

Jesus warned against even causing another to stumble on their journey to eternity. We are to be

careful of any practice or behavior that might cause
another to sin. Our example is to be consistent to
believer and sinner alike. In Romans we are reminded
that if we are even eating or drinking anything that
would cause another to stumble, it is sin (Romans
14:21-23). We are to be careful to bear up the weak
(Romans 15:1).

THE MESSAGE OF THE MILLSTONE

Jesus used a vivid word picture for people of His
day to emphasize His message of being careful to be a
proper example to those around us. The millstone was
part of the most important kitchen appliance in biblical
times. If the mill was not working, the family did not
eat. The stones ground the grain that was used for their
dietary staple — bread.

The mill utilized two stones. Each stone was
approximately two feet in diameter and six inches thick,
too heavy to be lifted on its own. The grinding process
often required the use of several slaves or oxen as the
stones were too heavy to move.

Jesus used the millstone example in three of the
gospels.

> **But whoso shall offend one of these little ones
> which believe in me, it were better for him that a
> millstone were hanged about his neck, and that he
> were drowned in the depth of the sea.**
>
> **Matthew 18:6**

Some believe "little ones" in this passage define
children since earlier in verse 3, Jesus is addressing
becoming as little children. Mark uses the same words,

but the message seems more clearly directed at those who are young in the faith, or new believers perhaps. When the Word admonishes parents not to provoke their children to wrath, I believe it covers the issue of our example in caring for the spiritual well-being and even mental health of the children God has placed in our charge.

Luke recorded the millstone story, as Jesus addressed the issue of responding to offense. We will be offended, Jesus said, but in return, we are not to cause others to stumble by becoming offensive ourselves (Luke 17:1,2). In doing so, we would be better off dead, He said, and drowned with a heavy millstone hung around our neck. What an indictment!

If you truly long for God and are passionate for His presence, you will be full of care for others. Dwelling with God will cause you to *think like Him*, to *care like Him*, to *react like Him*.

SPITE AND PASSION DON'T MIX

A backbiter is not in a passionate relationship with God. You don't have to be a Supreme Court Justice to make that ruling. It will be obvious by their words. A backbiter speaks spitefully about someone with the intent to inflict pain, usually because he or she is full of pain himself/herself.

A spiteful person wants to humiliate another. Causing someone else to hurt will never resolve personal pain, however. It simply increases that pain. Backbiting reveals a lack of care and compassion. Romans 1:30 lists backbiting as one of the acts of unrighteousness. It is an obvious act of one who is *not* in right standing with God.

DOING NO EVIL

The word *evil* conjures up all kinds of mental pictures. It is difficult to think of believers in Christ as operating in evil practices. However, the dictionary sheds some interesting light on that word. Its history demonstrates a relationship with the words over, up, under and beneath. In earlier times evil probably was simply "exceeding proper bounds."

Today the word is defined as anything morally wrong or bad which causes injury, ruin or pain. Often marked by anger or spite, it causes harm, misfortune or destruction. Spiritually speaking, anything that exists outside the boundaries of God's love and Jesus' earthly example could be called evil.[1]

Evil is commonplace in our society. We are confronted with evil on a daily basis. The conflict of good vs. evil is the basis for everything from the latest action movie, to the soap opera, to the nightly sitcom. The news is filled with wars, cops and criminals, murder and mayhem, all resulting from someone going beyond the boundaries of decent behavior.

Politicians take sides, pointing fingers at the other faction as the evil ones. The lines have been drawn, erased and redrawn so many times that it seems no one even knows where the true line is anymore. We have forgotten the original standard — The Word of God.

We have adopted situational ethics, a different standard for each circumstance. It is considered evil and it is a crime to kill an infant one minute after birth, yet it is perfectly legal to murder that same child anytime in the previous nine months of his or her life. You can be imprisoned for breaking a child's limb or bruising that child. From the womb, however, a child can be suctioned limb from limb, or drowned in saline solution and it is perfectly within the limits of the law.

The Bible is no longer the standard for right living. Even the precious Ten Commandments have been ordered off the wall of courtrooms in deference to the separation of Church and state argument. The Church did not set the standard. God set the standard, the same God whose name appears on our currency.

Money is used by everyone, atheist and Christian alike. Every time it is spent, it declares trust in God. Now here is a new argument for you. If there should be separation of Church and state, then why should we pay taxes with money that declares our faith and trust in God? Once again, the boundaries are reestablished to fit the circumstance.

When Eve ate of the tree in the garden of Eden, it was the tree of knowledge of good and evil (Genesis 2:9). Until this time man had known only good, now mankind would know the difference between good and evil. There would be lines drawn with laws given for protection. Once the door had been opened to evil, boundaries had to be set. God was the ultimate authority. It was He Who created good, therefore He alone could set the standard.

The standard was set not for God's good, but for the good of mankind — for protection and peaceful living. It was the original "Father Knows Best" production!

Romans 12:9 reminds us to abhor evil and cleave to what is good, yet today we are entertained by evil. We pay money to watch evil in action — murder, adultery and fornication. We have conditioned ourselves to accept the world's view as our new standard. The Scripture admonishes us not even to discuss what people do in darkness:

> **And have no fellowship with the unfruitful works of darkness, but rather reprove them.**
>
> **For it is a shame even to speak of those things which are done of them in secret**
>
> **Ephesians 5:11,12**

Yet we invest our time and money to watch Hollywood glorify acts of the flesh.

We no longer sense shame over unwed motherhood. We have told ourselves it is better than abortion. Often, we applaud the choice made to have the child, ignoring the fact that the wrong choice was made before conception. We have confused forgiveness and acceptance. Again, so many lines have been drawn that we have lost sight of the original boundary of God's standards.

We must once again begin to pray as Jesus taught us, "...deliver us from evil" (Matthew 6:13). Yes, there is balance in that we must love the sinner and hate the sin. Far too often we accept the sin and the sinner alike. We want to rely so heavily on God's grace that we omit any memory of His judgment.

Evil is not a sin of the world alone. The New Testament churches were continually admonished against speaking, doing or thinking evil. How much more then must we be on guard against the evils of our day.

THE BATTLE IS RAGING

It is the responsibility of the Church of the living

God to "...overcome evil with good" (Romans 12:21). It is a war and if you check the news, good hasn't taken much new ground lately. This alone should be reason enough to bring the Church to her knees in repentance. We should be crying out to God, "Deliver us, Father. Help us once again to raise the standard — to reestablish the line that separates good from evil and holiness from hellishness."

TABLOID CHRISTIANITY

David finally gets to the end of the hard-hitting verse 3 of Psalm, chapter 15, in his description of a righteous man — one who does not take up reproach against his neighbor. Webster not only defines *neighbor* as one who lives close by, but also as a fellow human being. I guess that just about takes in the whole wide world.

The standard set by the world is, "Anything goes, nothing is sacred." Tabloids and gossip shows pay big bucks for the latest inside sordid details of the lives of celebrities, political figures and religious leaders. Common folks play well too when caught in an uncommon act — the more heinous the better.

It is now the norm to find one's private life exposed to a national or worldwide audience through the media. Of course, evil sells. Once again we find ourselves entertained by the human failings of another. It somehow helps us feel better about our own struggle with evil. We don't seem quite so bad in light of all the really BAD guys out there.

When we use the world as the standard, we don't have to reach too high. God won't care that you felt you lived a little more righteous than an adulterous president, an alcoholic politician, a drug-abusing actor, a perverted senator, or an affluent baby killer. **They are not your standard for righteousness.**

When David warned against taking up a reproach, he was speaking against assessing blame, or bringing shame or disgrace on someone. Most of us are too godly to start something about our neighbor on our own, but we haven't had a standard to prohibit repeating another's slanderous remarks.

What kind of a standard makes us feel better about ourselves when a brother in Christ trips or falls? How much more value do we feel we have to God when someone who has raised millions of dollars to propagate the Gospel falls into sin? Where have we gotten the idea that sitting reproachfully in our pew, giving our $10 offering will mean anything to God?

Each man will give account for his own actions when he stands before God (Romans 14:12). I will not be able to justify my failures by the reproach of others. When the disciples came to Jesus complaining about the actions of others, Jesus admonished them, "...what is that to thee? follow thou me" (John 21:22).

It is time for the Church to be above reproach. As we continue to study the characteristics of the righteous and perfect man in Psalm 15, we learn what we must do to live above reproach. In this particular passage however, our attention is drawn to the importance of refusing to listen to, read, watch, or perpetuate in any way the stories of reproach about our neighbor. If inquiring minds really want to know, they should inquire of the Lord.

LET'S TALK ABOUT JESUS

The next time you are tempted to assess blame, backbite or repeat the tale of someone's shameful act — STOP. If you really desire to live and abide in God, then choose to talk about Jesus. Don't read the tabloid transcript of someone's extra-marital experience. Instead, pick up the Word of God and read about David's redemption from that sin.

If you are wanting a little action and adventure, follow the saga of Saul's jealousy of David. Let Saul's encounter with the witch of Endor teach you and keep you from seeking your word from God through the psychic hot line.

By the world's standards it may appear that sin offers some great rewards — an Oscar, or an Emmy, a gold record, wealth, fame, a photo on the cover of a national magazine. The Bible gives the price of sin in black and white — "...the wages of sin is death" (Romans 6:23).

God's standard is high. Those willing to treat their neighbor with care by refusing to backbite, by resisting evil doing, and by rejecting any opportunities to bring reproach, are taking some of the most important steps toward living and dwelling forever in God's presence.

KEY 2
WATCHFUL

2
WATCHFUL

In whose eyes a vile person is contemned; but he honoureth them that fear the Lord.

Psalm 15:4a

In children's church years ago you could hear the refrain of a little song with a big message: "Be careful little eyes what you see...." This is still an important word for today. Our eyes are continually bombarded with the actions of the vile.

Webster defines *vile* as "morally despicable or abhorrent (nothing is so as intellectual dishonesty); physically repulsive; mean; tending to degrade; disgustingly or utterly bad."[2]

Vile people operate in the objectionable and disgusting. They cannot seem to satisfy their taste for the things that are abominable, wretched and depraved. You may think David was talking to the ungodly in this passage, yet more and more we are seeing vile things played out in the Church family.

We have allowed ourselves to become blinded by the actions of our vile brothers and sisters, because they are part of our fellowship. We have refused to see. We no longer ask God for discernment when we have observed something that seems to be out of the ordinary in behavior. Our spiritual eyes refuse to look at things in the light of God's Word that may be evident even to people of the world.

Without using discernment, a pastor hires a choir director who has left his previous position amid charges of sexual abuse of an eleven-year-old boy. The pastor fails to recognize, through the Spirit, the vile person's actions. In "faith" he takes the word of the choir director without taking literally the Word of God. When a young boy in that pastor's congregation is molested, the pastor is shocked and angry that the man lied, but it is too late. Another precious life has been scarred.

An evangelist comes to your church and keeps to himself. He leaves the housing you have provided in the middle of the night to "get some air." You believe that something is wrong, but he will be out of town in a few days so it is not your problem. Someone even brings a report that their brother saw someone in a ball cap who looked a lot like your evangelist having a drink in an all-night bar during the wee hours of the morning. You ignore the report and invite him back for next year. After all, people were moved and the offerings were good. It was probably a case of mistaken identity. This man is God's responsibility!

Your son's grades are suffering. Often, you have to make him go to church on Sunday, but he goes. You think you noticed a strange bittersweet smell coming from his room when you had been out of the house one evening, but you were too tired and busy to put it under the microscope of God's Word. After all, he is eighteen now and by summer he'll be out on his own. What you don't know won't hurt you, right?

Your friend takes you to great places for lunch and she always picks up the check. Last year she bought you that great blouse for your birthday, one you could never afford. You like her outgoing manner and how she seems to know everyone. It is fun to meet the important people. She knows all the bigwigs in your denomination and goes to all the conferences.

Every time you are with her, you learn something new and disgusting about someone you admired. She seems to delight in knowing and repeating the most vile reports, always under the guise of, "We need to pray for so-and-so." Think about it. When was the last time you actually prayed with her for someone?

You need to run to the grocery store. Your husband's car is parked behind yours in the driveway and he's mowing the lawn, so you grab his keys and run out for the quick stop. Your wallet drops from your lap onto the car floor. Reaching for it, you notice a magazine sticking out from under the driver's seat. Thumbing through it, you find the material shocking. You had never imagined such deplorable sexual acts, and here they are jumping from the pages in living color.

In a daze you run into the quick stop, grab the milk you needed and fall back into your husband's vehicle. Sitting there stunned, you visualize him in your mind standing before the Sunday school class teaching about communion. That was one of his best lessons. You see him passing the offering plate, proudly displaying the perfect attendance pin on his lapel. You see yourself driving the kids home after service, because he has to stay for an all-important board meeting. But this new information does not compute.

Does this make him less of a husband or father? He still teaches with great conviction. People are always affirming his teaching. He never misses a church service. He is a good provider and a responsible elder in the church. You drive home slowly, put dinner on the table and complain of a headache. You head for bed. After all, things will look brighter in the morning.

It is time to stop passing the buck, looking the other way and ignoring the obvious. Sin is sin and it is time to call it by its name. God was ready to destroy Nineveh for its vile actions (Nahum 1:14), but it is important to remember, first He sent them a redemption message.

GOD, DON'T GIVE UP ON ME!

In his writing to the church at Rome, Paul had some strong words regarding God's position against vile acts. In verse 21 of Romans, chapter 1, we are made aware that the people being referred to knew and recognized God as God, yet they did not honor and glorify Him as God.

We are taught we must glorify God with our whole body and spirit, which are His (1 Corinthians 6:20). Anything less is the same as failing to glorify Him at all.

> **For this reason God gave them over and abandoned them to vile affections and degrading passions. For their women exchanged their natural function for anunnatural and abnormal one,**
>
> **And the men also turned from natural relations with women and were set ablaze (burning out, consumed) with lust for one another — men committing shameful acts with men and suffering in their own bodies and personalities the inevitable**

consequences and penalty of their wrongdoing and going astray, which was [their] fitting retribution.

And so, since they did not see fit to acknowledge God or approve of Him or consider Him worth the knowing, God gave them over to a base and condemned mind to do things not proper or decent but loathsome,

Until they were filled (permeated and saturated) with every kind of unrighteousness, iniquity, grasping and coveteous greed, and malice. [They were] full of envy and jealousy, murder, strife, deceit and treachery, ill will and cruel ways. [They were] secret backbiters and gossipers,

Slanderers, hateful to and hating God, full of insolence, arrogance, [and] boasting; inventors of new forms of evil, disobedient and undutiful to parents.

[They were] without understanding, conscienceless and faithless, heartless and loveless [and] merciless.

Though they are fully aware of God's righteous decree that those who do such things deserve to die, they not only do themselves but approve and applaud others who practice them.

Romans 1:26-32 AMP

VILE PRACTICES

Paul details vile practices, leaving no room for questions. With the recent revelation of a comedienne sitcom star's sexual preference, only one religious leader has gone public with an outcry against the sin of homosexuality. Many of us have not wanted to be a part of his camp since we have observed some of his actions to be too radical. Further, we have not always viewed his actions as completely honorable in previous dealings, actions as completely honorable in previous dealings, so we have pulled away from his philosophy and have failed to take a stand against evil.

The enemy of our soul may be blinding us with the actions of the messenger and in doing so, attempting to water down the message which is straight from the Word of God. Homosexuality is a sin. It is an abomination to God, and we must be watchful while loving the sinner that we do not begin to tolerate the sin. When we accept and applaud those entrenched in the sin of homosexuality, we are approving their behavior. Instead we should be weeping before God, crying out for the souls of those bound by Satan's schemes.

Perhaps the key to this entire passage is the word *desire*. Man's passionate desire for pleasure makes him do all sorts of things. It seems strange to think of God abandoning anyone as Paul refers to in verse 28 of Romans, chapter 1. When we see all the evil in the earth and are tempted to ask God why, the answer is in the free will God gave us.

God gave us a free will, therefore He respects man's ability to choose. When God abandons men to uncleanness, the word *abandon* has no angry irritation in it. It is not even condemnation and judgment, but wistful, sorrowful regret. It describes exactly the feeling of the father when he saw his son turn his back on his home and go out to a far country.[3]

The judgment that comes into play in these circumstances is immediate. It is an opening of a door to every evil work, and sin begets sin. Paul knew the wages of sin was more than judgment in the afterlife. It was living in and propagating sin, sending it into coming generations.

A Reprobate Mind

When God gave up on men who lived in or laughed at sin, they were no longer able to have the mind of Christ, but possessed a reprobate mind. Webster's dictionary defines *reprobate* as "one who is morally unprincipled."[4] I believe we have many in the church today who are not practicing immorality, but they are subconsciously accepting it, bit by bit into their lives.

It is difficult to watch even one television show without encountering some reference to immorality, which we now find the object of humor. We call it entertainment when two beautiful young sitcom stars fight over the one remaining condom in the house, and one of the unmarried girls has to go without sex for the evening because of it.

Acts which used to be unspeakable are now comedy material for family viewing. Effeminate men and masculine women are presented as normal contributing members of society and gradually we are beginning to accept this lie in the name of equality. Oh yes, we laugh at their antics and their dress, we laugh when we should be turning our heads in shame, or better yet turning our television sets off and getting on our faces before God.

Entertained By Sin

The very things God hates we now find entertaining. We actually pay money to see movies that violate all of the Ten Commandments in a few fleeting moments. If we are too holy to go to the theater, then we rent the videos and watch them at home, allowing filth and violence to become part of our thinking process. We are no longer horrified by the spilling of blood. News shows have to be more graphic to maintain their audience's need for gore. We may only watch the edited version of violence played on the network, but we are compromising just the same.

The report of a scientific study, recently released on the national news, indicates that we actually have more free time now than did previous generations, yet we are too busy to be in the house of the Lord. The television is viewed an average of seven hours a day in the households of America according to NBC Nightly News. How long has it been since you spent seven hours in one day passionately seeking the presence of the Lord?

Obvious Actions of Unrighteousness

Let's examine the Greek words and definitions of several areas of unrighteousness:

Fornication, *porneia*, refers to unlawful sex sins of single and married people. These sins are unlawful in God's eyes only, because existing laws against adultery, sodomy, and fornication in this country are now considered antiquated.

Wickedness, *poneria*, means to act in an evil nature; criminal behavior.

Covetousness, *pleonexia*, means intense lust for gain.

Maliciousness, *kakia*, means vicious disposition and desires — simply having them. This does not include acting them out.

Envy, *phthonos*, means pain or displeasure felt when seeing another person being blessed.

Murder, *phonos*, means actual slaughter, but also includes hating another person.

Debate, *eris*, means strife, or causing strife or discord.

Deceit, *dolos*, includes lying, falsity, operating openly or subtly or craftily.

Malignity, *kakoetheia*, is a disposition that produces evil habits. It means malignity of the mind, which leads its victim to put the worst construction on every action, ascribing to the best deeds the worst motives.

Whisperers, *psithuristes*, means secret detractors who pretend secrecy and carry out accusations against men, whether true or false, blasting their reputation by gossip.

Backbiters, *katalolos*, includes evil speakers, false accusers, slanderers of absent men.

Haters of God, *theostuges*, means hateful to God, not only atheists, but condemners of sacred things, despisers of providence, scorners of good.

Despiteful, *hubristes*, means insolent; stormy; boisterous; abusing the characters of those under them; scornful; hateful.

Proud, *huperephanos*, means to indulge in pride or self-gratulation, be exalted; glory in self, display or strut self before others; undue sense of superiority, unnatural self-esteem; arrogance; wishing all men to receive their sayings as law.

Boasters, *alazon*, means self-exalted, vain and arrogant braggarts.

Inventors of evil, *epheuretes*, means originators of wicked, immoral and sinful customs, rites, and fashions; beginners of the abominable religious orgies; degrading shows of the theater, and the gambling tables.

Disobedient to parents involves indifference to rule and order; irreverent.

Without understanding means ignorant and destitute of capacity for spiritual things; stubborn.

Covenant breakers, *asunthetos*, means not morally bound to any agreement; not dependable, treacherous to covenants; faithless to promises; false to trusts.

Without natural affection, means to be filled with desire for unnatural affection experiences with husband or wife or same sex partners and other deviation sins.

Implacable, *aspondos*, means one who cannot be appeased or pacified by God; unforgiving spirit; will not reconcile with God or man.

Unmerciful, *aneleemon*, means destitute of all benevolence to the needy, cruel, merciless.[5]

Examine Yourself

That is an amazing list of "shortcomings." Do we see any of these things that have slipped into our thinking or behavior? I am certain we identified many other people involved in some of these areas of sin as we read the list.

It is true, *we must first examine ourselves.* How have we let the patterns of the world change our thinking? What associations have we made which may have caused us to justify thoughts or actions that are not like Jesus? What steps can we take to be different?

ESTHER'S EXAMPLE

The Scripture offers some helpful hints in separating ourselves from those with vile influence over our lives. In the third chapter of Esther we find a godly man, Mordecai, refusing to bow or do reverence to the evil Haman.

Haman was under the influence of evil and in an all out personal war against the Jews. He had connived to exalt himself. He was in a position to be worshipped, but Mordecai refused to bow down to him. Mordecai had his spiritual eyes open and he recognized the satanic attack. He was watchful of the evil and refused to show respect to the vile.

When Mordecai refused to bow down and worship Haman, he [Haman] launched an attack on the entire Jewish race. Again, he plotted to completely destroy God's chosen people.

But Mordecai had a plan. The same plan, if implemented today, would still be effective. Mordecai humbled himself and cried out to God. He fasted and prayed, as did all of the Jews he influenced. When Queen Esther heard the plan, she called her staff to prayer and fasting as well. The challenge was now before her to do what she could to effect a change in the king's order which allowed Haman to do this evil deed.

Esther prayed and fasted for God's direction and favor with the king. Even though she was not certain if she would be received by him, she put her life on the line. Her cause was great, it was for freedom from the evil edict against God's people. Esther had to stand against the evil that was operating with the approval of the king.

With the prayer covering and a fresh dose of holy boldness, Esther was able to take her cause before King Ahasuerus. The former order was amended and the Jews were able to fight off the ungodly attempt to destroy them. Once Haman had been put to death for his deceitful role, Esther made one more request — one that may seem a little unusual to us today.

Queen Esther had all the descendants of the wicked Haman put to death. She allowed nothing to remain of the ungodly seed. She made certain that chain of evil was not only broken but obliterated.

Once the ties have been cut with someone who habitually practices evil, it is very important to permanently close the door. Burn the bridges or do whatever it takes to insure that relationship has no further or future hold on you.

It may seem radical but when another individual has given himself or herself over to Satan for his use in evil operation, you will have no need of any fellowship there again. If at some time in the future the person repents, it would be up to God to birth a new relationship. The person with a true passion for the presence of God does not call holy or associate with anything that God calls unholy.

GIVING HONOR WHERE HONOR IS DUE

David emphasized giving honor to those who are serving the Lord. The dictionary describes *honor* as esteem or respect, even reverence for position.

**Be devoted to one another in brotherly love.
Honor one another above yourselves.**

Romans 12:10 NIV

**The elders who direct the affairs of the church
well are worthy of double honor, especially those
whose work is preaching and teaching.**

1 Timothy 5:17 NIV

It is crucial to be discerning when it comes to evil,
and it is equally important to recognize the goodness
that comes from God. When we discern good in others,
we should show them honor. We are often more critical
of those who labor among us and are doing good than
of those who are operating in evil.

Simply paying the preacher or Christian worker is
not giving them honor. They are anointed and called of
God and if they have been faithful in their service to
Him, then they are worthy of any honor that can be
given to them.

Any evil report that should reach us about the one
who is laboring in the Word or in the doctrine should
only be heard if there is more than one witness. We
should always believe the best until proven otherwise.
How long has it been since you honored someone who
has been faithful in bringing the Word to you? Perhaps
you feel simply giving your tithes and offerings is all
that you need to do.

When you tithe, you are giving to the work of
the Lord, but what about the workman? Have you told
him or her how much they mean to you? Have you
shared a testimony of spiritual growth because of their
ministry? There are many ways to let someone know
you honor and esteem them in the Lord.

Be watchful of those who labor among you. Study
their lives and learn from their example. Ask God to
give you creative ways to bless and encourage them in

their ministry. As you bless them, they will bless you. When a person feels appreciated, they will work harder and give more. Shower them with love and appreciation, and it will come back to you in abundant and surprising ways.

Don't forget to honor all those workers who give so generously of their time with no salary. Bless them at every opportunity. Pour good into their lives.

When we as a body of believers truly begin to honor one another, the world will be drawn to us. We may have our differences, but we are each a part of the same body.

WHAT PART ARE YOU?

Consider the story of the foot. Now the foot has had a hard day. It often does. You see, the foot is stuffed into a sock and crammed into a run-down shoe. All day it has had to carry the full weight of all the other body parts. By evening the foot is tired, not to mention sweaty and smelly. The nose is not happy with the smelly foot, even though all day it carried around that sniffling nose.

The leg tried to support the foot all day, but now it has a muscle cramp. The stomach is a little queazy because the foot took it to a terrible place for lunch. The head is pounding because all the parts of the body seem to be complaining about something.

The head decides that the entire body should just sit down and regroup. The back informs the head that it would feel better if it were soaked in a hot tub and for the first time that day the entire body is in agreement. This will benefit all of them.

After a hot bath the body is dried off by the arm, though it felt the bath didn't last long enough. The head makes another decision to rest the body on the couch. Sitting quietly, the body really does not want to move and yet the foot is still throbbing from its daily duty.

Without fuss or fanfare, the torso leans forward, the arm reaches for the food and the hand gently begins to massage the weary, aching foot. The mouth sighs in comfort and the eyes close in relief. Someone is ministering to the foot. Someone is honoring the foot's hard day of work. The leg cramp loosens and the head simply marvels at the ability of the body to minister to itself — to ease another's burden — to honor the labor of another part.

God created the body to work in harmony — one part with another — then He called the Church His Body. We must recognize the work of every part and honor each participant. The entire body would go nowhere, except for the work of the foot. The head got all the attention all day long, but someone took the time to honor the foot.

Begin to recognize all the parts in the Body of Christ as significant. Perhaps it is time to give honor to the elbow — the one who is always bending and flexible, perhaps lifting and setting up chairs for events, then storing them away again.

Maybe you need to honor the knee, the one who is always bending in prayer for the meetings and the needs of the people. Perhaps your healing or present prosperity is due to the prayers of that "bended knee." The knee might have a need you could meet if you simply sought God for a way to honor the faithfulness.

As a Body, we cannot function without the help of each other. Giving honor to one part can only benefit the entire being, bringing it to greater health and wholeness. Ask God to help you this week to honor someone in your congregation or ministry family. When you have a true passion for the presence of God, *you will begin to recognize the value of others.* You will begin to see the entire Body through the eyes of Jesus.

KEY 3
FAITHFUL

3

FAITHFUL

...He that sweareth to his own hurt, and changeth
not.

Psalm 15:4b

In today's language this passage would probably
be interpreted as "one who keeps his word even when
it hurts." Jesus kept His word to the Father when He
went to the cross. He would have preferred not to
endure it, but He was assured of the joy that was set
before Him (Hebrews 12:2). He even cried out to God,
if it were possible, He would like to pass on the Calvary
experience (Luke 22:42).

Keeping your word, even when it hurts, is almost
a lost art today. We now have situational ethics. We lie
to ourselves, to our children, to our employers, to the
government and to God — but He knows the truth. The
wisest man who ever lived, Solomon, said that it would
be better to be poor than to be a liar (Proverbs 19:22).

The devil is the father of lies (John 8:44). When
he first encountered Eve, he caused her to question
God's Word by asking if God really said if they ate of
the tree they would die (Genesis 3:1). The devil only
operates in deceit, for the truth is not in him. He twists
and perverts everything to suit his selfish purposes.

When you are passionately seeking the presence of God, you will not be speaking in the language of lies. There is an old joke that asks the question, "How can you tell if a man is lying?" The answer is, "If his mouth is open." Unfortunately, this has become too true about mankind.

If you stopped just now and took a survey of the people you know, how many would you find who are always faithful to their word?

We know that all liars will have their place in the lake of fire (Revelation 3:8), yet that doesn't stop us from being faithless to our word. We no longer fear hell.

We could argue that in **most** things we are faithful to our word. After all, we know what is important to God and we are faithful to our word when it comes to those things. God knows our heart and He really understands when we fail to follow through with our promises — that's not really lying.

God's Word declares that if we are faithful in the small things, He will make us ruler over many things (Matthew 25:23). It is the little foxes that spoil the vine (Song of Solomon 2:15), and we will have to give an account when we stand before God of every idle word we speak (Matthew 12:36,37). That doesn't leave much room for doubt about the necessity for integrity in keeping our word, even to our own hurt.

LYING IS CONTAGIOUS

Abraham was a man of God. He heard God's voice and usually obeyed. When Abraham became afraid that he would lose his wife, he lied to Pharaoh, saying that

Sarah was his sister (Genesis 12:11-20). It seems harmless enough, a little white lie perhaps.

It may seem important to look at the reasons why Abraham lied, but if we could explain it, would that matter to God? God is not interested in the reason. He is not a God of situational ethics. He was big enough to protect Sarah. Abraham did not need to trust in a lie. Abraham only needed to trust in God.

Isaac learned from his father. He was raised in the ways of God. He had seen God spare his life and provide a sacrificial ram in his place (Genesis 22:1-18). Isaac felt the need to lie about his wife Rebekah, and say that she was his sister. He too was afraid (Genesis 26:7). How is it that he had not yet learned to trust God with his wife, when he had trusted God with his own life?

Jacob learned from his father. He lied out of greed. He wanted the birthright. He wanted the blessing. He was a deceiver and his mother assisted him in being deceitful (Genesis 27).

Children learn what they live. If we are under the influence of the father of lies, then we pass that influence on. Generations come and generations go and the lying spirit is perpetuated.

Parents are often shocked when their children are caught in some big lie. They simply cannot imagine where their precious youngster got the idea. Perhaps they heard their father call in sick one day last week when he was really staying home to paint the house. Maybe his mother told him to say she was not home when an annoying friend called.

When a parent gives a child his or her promise

about something and then does not fulfill that promise, that is a lie. It may seem justifiable since "something just came up," but to that child it is a lie. Mom and Dad have not been faithful to their word.

Unfortunately, we have changed the name of lies to excuses. We have tried to water down the impact of that sin. We cheat (lie) on our taxes because the government already gets too much of our money. Every day people sign papers committing to an agreement they know they will never fulfill.

Couples marry, make vows and then forget to be faithful to their word. "Till death do us part," has come to mean "until I wish you were dead because I can't stand you anymore."

Several years ago an interesting book reported some sad findings. As I read *The Day America Told the Truth*, I found much of its information shocking. When Americans were asked who they trusted least — who were the most dishonest people they knew — television evangelists ranked above used car dealers.[6]

We are no longer shocked when we hear reports that our President has lied. Most Americans believe the government has not told them the truth about many national and international issues. We care so little for the truth we are willing to read any scandal sheet that reports anything negative about anyone famous, or infamous as the case might be.

A SAD STATE OF AFFAIRS

Many books written during and after a recent highly publicized trial, point fingers at others who lied.

Everyone wanted to make their point of view known. Many were convinced that O. J. lied, but truth could not be found so all the players began to accuse each other of lying.

Lawyers blasted lawyers, lawyers blamed judges, lawyers accused witnesses, witnesses mistrusted other witnesses, police investigators turned on one another, friends lied about each other, and families are still accusing families of lying for personal gain.

Much money was made in the telling of each fragmented side of the tale, but the consequences have been most severe in that we no longer trust our criminal justice system. We have little or no respect for those who are to protect and preserve our freedoms. We watch and read with morbid curiosity, all the while wondering, "Who do you trust? Is anyone faithful to his word?"

Two Sides to Every Story

We have come to believe that there are indeed two sides to every story. It is all a matter of perspective. It has been decided somewhere along the line that either we look at a glass as being half full or half empty. However, both perspectives have merit.

Our view of a situation can be tainted by many different experiences from our past life, but we must draw the line and refuse to allow any more compromise when it comes to the choice between right and wrong. For the Christian there are no gray areas. We have tried hard to straddle the fence on so many issues. We have wanted to blend rather than make waves. Our greatest sin perhaps has been in lying to ourselves.

TELLING YOURSELF THE TRUTH

Try talking to yourself. Yes, others may accuse you of being crazy, but it is about time you sat yourself down for a reality check. How long have you been lying to yourself? Truth therapy doesn't have to be a complicated process. It just requires rigorous honesty, plain common sense and a desire to improve your life and your relationships with God and man.[7]

If you are not first true to yourself, how can you be honest with others? Since I am not a psychiatrist, I cannot begin to walk you through the process of facing the real issues of your life. I can, however, introduce you to the Great Physician Who created you and has the power to recreate anything in you that is not in sync with His standards.

We need to throw ourselves at His feet and cry out for mercy. He has promised to teach us all things (John 14:26). With God's help we can begin to see the truth within us through the light of His Word.

We have been making excuses (lying) for too long. We have blamed our past for our present attitudes. No one wants to take personal responsibility for their bad behavior. It has to be our mother's fault, our father's, our abuser's, a former mate's or a previous employer's fault. No one wants to admit they are just hateful, resentful, jealous, bitter or angry because they choose to be. But moment by moment, we make those choices daily, then lie to ourselves about them.

Certainly we must deal with the crisis situations of our lives which have colored our dispositions, but it's time to forget those things which are behind and press toward the mark of the prize of the high calling of God in Christ Jesus (Philippians 3:13,14). It will go a long way toward our healing and wholeness. We are greatly in need of a fresh baptism in the Spirit of Truth.

You might not know why you do the things you do. Sometimes when people come to me repeatedly with the same behavior problems, I want to say, "Just stop it!" In every circumstance you have a choice. Make the right one. Choose truth.

Stop lying to yourself. Take a giant step toward truth and Jesus will meet you.

PRAY AND PAY

Walking in truth will require divine assistance. We live in a hostile environment where truth is rarely honored. To break free from past patterns, you will need to passionately pursue God's presence. Truth is found in His presence, but it is expensive — it will cost you something. If you want to dwell in His tabernacle, you must be willing to pay the price.

Part of that price is, telling the truth will hurt your flesh. It won't make you popular or famous. John the Baptist told the truth and it cost him his head!

WHO ELSE ARE YOU LYING TO?

It may seem hard to believe but you would be amazed at the number of people I see who actually lie to God. It must be a big joke in heaven when an all-seeing, all-knowing God hears a lie from one of His kids.

God hates lying (Psalm 119:163). It is a real waste of time and energy. Why not just throw your silly self at

His feet and beg for mercy and forgiveness for your stupidity? He knows exactly what you did and why you did it. He is God, you know. I am reminded of one of Carman's great songs that says plainly, "God doesn't want your big ol' song and dance, He just wants your faith and trust in Him."

God is not impressed with your "creativity" or your ability to speak the devil's language. He doesn't want to hear it. He just wants you to get real with Him.

In Acts 5, we have a scenario of a husband and wife lying to the Holy Ghost. Death was the result:

> But a certain man named Ananias, with Sapphira his wife, sold a possession,
>
> And kept back part of the price, his wife also being privy to it, and brought a certain part, and laid it at the apostles' feet.
>
> But Peter said, Ananias, why hath Satan filled thine heart to lie to the Holy Ghost, and to keep back part of the price of the land?
>
> Whiles it remained, was it not thine own? and after it was sold, was it not in thine own power? why hast thou conceived this thing in thine heart? thou hast not lied unto men, but unto God.
>
> And Ananias hearing these words fell down, and gave up the ghost: and great fear came on all them that heard these things.
>
> Acts 5:1-5

Sapphira, the wife of Ananias, repeated the process. She lied and dropped dead as well (v. 10). Lying to God **is** deadly. These ignorant folks lied when the truth would have been fine. They weren't required to give all the proceeds of the sale of their property. The "pride factor" was operating and they were probably determined to keep up with the Jones's who had given their all.

The pride factor is still active today! You can find it alive and well in services where the speaker asks fifty people to stand and give a thousand dollars. I have counted those offerings and then counted the returned checks from those wishing to look good to the congregation, when in fact, they knew they were unable to fulfil such a commitment.

We may think we really don't have to worry about an Ananias and Sapphira event happening today. In the modern church we don't see any liars dropping dead, or do we?

> Therefore, whoever eats the bread or drinks the cup of the Lord in an unworthy manner will be guilty of sinning against the body and blood of the Lord. A man ought to examine himself before he eats of the bread and drinks of the cup. For anyone who eats and drinks without recognizing the body of the Lord eats and drinks judgment on himself. That is why many among you are weak and sick, and a number of you have fallen asleep.
>
> 1 Corinthians 11:27-30 NIV

Someone once said that the most hypocritical hour of the week is Sunday morning between 11 and 12 noon. They were right on target. We stand and sing, "I Surrender All" and "Take Your Burdens to the Cross and Leave Them There." Before we reach the back door, we've picked them all back up. Our plan is to take them home and somehow work them out during the next week.

We say Amen when the minister encourages tithing, then drop an empty giving envelope into the offering plate just to look good. We can't wait to get to lunch so we can criticize the song leader or the mismatched outfit of the pianist. Everyone else is a hypocrite! (But it takes one to know one!)

When we are encouraged to raise our hands in praise we follow directions, but our hands lie. They are raised, but inside we are planning where to go to lunch or how to avoid that deacon who always wants to chat after church. When the communion elements are passed we have no problem with partaking, but we keep an eye out for anyone we perceive is taking it unworthily. Paul stated for this cause some have become sick and many have died (1 Corinthians 11:30).

I cannot begin to claim that all sickness and death in the Body of Christ is a result of sin. Only eternity will reveal the full extent of Paul's words to the Church. But this I do know: God hates liars. He keeps His Word, and one day there will be a judgment.

COUNT THE COST

For those who are willing to pay the price, the rewards are great. Salvation is free, but denying evil will cost your flesh everything. Complete surrender of every fiber of your being will be painful. Your flesh will rebel. Satan will throw in every obstacle to deter you as you journey to enter God's presence.

When Stephen was stoned, he had already paid the price. His flesh had long ago surrendered to the power of God. As Stephen faced the angry mob, he saw no man. He had no angry uprising. His eyes were on Jesus, Who was standing at the Father's right hand. Scripture says as he was being stoned to death, "...he kneeled down, and cried with a loud voice, Lord, lay not this sin to their charge. And when he had said this, he fell asleep" (Acts 7:60).

When you are faithful to God's Word, your word will also be trustworthy. Only truth can exist in His precious presence.

KEY 4
MERCIFUL

4
MERCIFUL

He that putteth not out his money to usury, nor taketh reward against the innocent....

Psalm 15:5a

As your passion for the presence of God opens the door to His tabernacle, you will find yourself operating in one of His greatest attributes — mercy. Remember, it did not take God long to become sickened with mankind. By chapter 5 of Genesis, God already had it with the wicked and He was ready to wash them off the face of the earth. I am thankful Noah found grace and mercy in the eyes of the Lord (Genesis 6:8).

God had mercy on self-centered Lot and his not-so-godly family, sparing them from the destruction of Sodom and Gomorrah. He had mercy on the rebellious children of Israel who preferred to worship a golden calf and complained every step of their deliverance journey.

Time and time again I believe God repented that He made man. If God ever questioned one of His own decisions, I would imagine more than once He would have questioned that "free will for man" thing!

GOD KEEPS HIS PROMISES

Long before David needed a megadose of mercy,

God promised it to him. God sent Nathan the prophet to David to give him some precious promises for the future. God told David that His mercy would not depart from him. How could God make such a promise when He was all-knowing? It wouldn't be long before David would commit adultery and order the death of his lover's husband. God knew that more than anything else, David would **need** mercy.

Later, David could easily sing of the mercies of the Lord. He knew firsthand about goodness and mercy that would follow him all the days of his life (Psalm 23:6). More than any other writer, David would constantly refer to the mercies of God. Even though he had been promised mercy, he often cried out to God for it. He knew what he needed and was not afraid to seek it. Perhaps he wanted to remind God of His promise.

David found mercy in the presence of God. When he was on the run, he often found himself drawing near to God in love and fellowship. He became so full of God at one point, he was called a man after God's own heart.

David was passionate about God. He pursued God. He went after the very heart of God. What he knew of God, he had come to love and he sought to be like Him.

The mercy of God operating in David was evident when he had the opportunity to kill Saul, yet walked away, leaving Saul in the hands of God (1 Samuel 24:1-12). He could have taken matters into his own hands, after all Saul had tried to kill him and was even then hunting him down. David made no attempt to justify such an action of the flesh, but operated in the mercy of God.

In this particular portion of Scripture, David uses

the example of one passionately seeking God. One longing to dwell in the tabernacle of God is merciful, he would not resort to usury.

Usury is the practice of loaning money at an exorbitant or illegal rate of interest.[8] One who does this is taking unfair advantage of someone in a condition of critical need. If a person was not in desperate need, he or she would never be persuaded to take out a loan at a ridiculously high rate of interest.

David's example is a simple one with much more meaning than is expressed in the short sentence. He is addressing anyone who would take advantage of the poor. You cannot take advantage if you don't have the advantage. A person becomes a victim when another has any type of power over his or her life. When you possess that power you can use it to manipulate or to show mercy.

POWER — THE FORCE BEHIND MANIPULATION

The world is familiar with manipulation. It is nothing new. The greed for power and position is as old as the universe. No one is surprised when a power broker gobbles up another company, dismantles it and puts thousands of people out of work in an attempt to gain more control in a certain market. Some even see that as business savvy. It is rewarded with some respect and a lot of reverent fear and awe of the skill.

Politicians use words to manipulate votes. They make extensive promises, exaggerate criticisms of the other candidates, all under the guise of making your city, state, or world a better place.

THE FIRST MANIPULATOR

The earliest recorded incident of manipulation was not done by a man. It was initiated by a spiritual being — the musician formerly known as Lucifer. You thought I was going to say prince. Well, Lucifer did become a prince — the prince of the power of the air.

Lucifer decided to take more control than God had given him and in his attempt manipulated one-third of the angels to join his camp. Don't forget Lucifer was the worship leader in heaven. He was beautiful and gifted and felt that should bring him more clout in the Kingdom.

Lucifer's revolution got him his own kingdom — the kingdom of darkness. I am certain that his kingdom wasn't quite as exciting as he had hoped, that is, until man came along. It was time to practice up on those old manipulating skills. He now had new territory to conquer, the hearts and minds of the children of God. What a playground this would be!

What a great opportunity. Here were these two young married people (Adam and Eve) with no heavenly history to combat. They had a little quiet time with God Who had dropped them in a comfortable place to live, gave them companionship and trusted them to do the right thing. After all, why wouldn't they? Everything had been provided for them and there was only one negative rule.

Scripture does not tell us how long the serpent actually took to beguile Eve. I believe he took his time. After all, he had aeons of time. Little by little he gained her trust. He made her rethink her place in her earthly and heavenly relationships. Slowly he manipulated her mind.

I don't believe for one minute that Eve was created gullible or stupid. She was created from Adam's side and he was the caretaker of every plant and animal in God's domain. He was no slouch. He had God-given degrees in zoology, botany and horticulture. He probably could have used a few classes in husbandry — the ones that taught him to keep his wife fulfilled in every way, including conversation. Perhaps then she would have had no need to make conversation with a serpent.

Sin blinded mankind to truth. Transgression opened the door to victimization. Man was created by God with power and privilege. Sin caused mankind's fall from that favored position.

From that day to this, man has played "follow the leader." Satan set the example and for most of earth, manipulation and control were and still are the name of his game.

As we have already discussed, the condition and the manipulation of man made God sick. Initially He just wanted to end the madness, but then He had a better idea. This one was perhaps even better than His original plan of sinless perfection. This would be the greatest demonstration of power, love and mercy.

What control God must have had. All power was His. He could have destroyed the earth and started over. Who would know? He would still come out looking like God.

In the continuing struggle for power by the prince, God's mercy was about to rewrite history. From the beginning of time God was secure in His plan for man. It was a plan for good and not for evil. It was now time to put the mercy plan into effect.

THE MERCIFUL SON — OUR SAVIOR

Jesus left the mercyseat and came to earth in the form of a baby. He lived among us and dealt with every human emotion. Most of the choices He had to make were not easy ones. Continually faced with threats of death, rejection, misunderstanding and misguided followers, He stood strong in His mission of mercy.

He knew His purpose. The Son of God made His way to an earth filled with sin and evil to shed His blood for the redemption of mankind. His mercy rewrote my history and yours.

I love the old hymn, "He Could Have Called Ten Thousand Angels." Jesus had the freedom to choose any path, any escape route, and yet He chose mercy for you and me. I don't know about you, but the depth of that truth makes me want to shout.

He had **all** power. Every fiber of His earthly being was in check. The Spirit of God was in control, and He chose to mercifully die for our sins. Jesus is our supreme example of mercy.

If we have been truly redeemed and His Spirit is living in us, then we will exhibit that same mercy toward others. We will not manipulate or take advantage of those in need or the less fortunate.

MANIPULATION IS NOT JUST A WORLDLY THING

Manipulation in the Church has reached an all-time high while seeking entrance into God's presence has reached an all-time low. We have forgotten the power that is available to us through Christ Jesus, and we have resorted to our own power source in an effort to control. Long before Burger King told us we could have it our way, right away we were insisting on it — at every turn.

We have become self-centered, self-focused and just plain selfish! We are into self-help for most everything, while our example was selfless and self-sacrificing. The Church often mirrors the world in its attempt to control and dominate. We were created to take dominion, yet we have lost sight of what we are to dominate.

We are to be the dominant force in the earth. We are to be the primary example of good. We've been wasting a lot of time and energy trying to dominate each other, and unfortunately, we have gotten pretty good at it. So good in fact, that often you cannot tell the Church from the world. God have mercy on us!

Manipulation is a form of witchcraft. Any time you seek to control or dominate the actions of others, you are a practicing witch. You might as well call some churches a coven.

THE JEZEBEL SPIRIT

The Jezebel spirit is alive and well and in operation in the Church. Jezebel was a scheming, shameless woman. She manipulated everyone from her husband to a nation. She infiltrated the Hebrews with her Phoenician gods. Joram charged her with the practice of witchcraft (2 Kings 9:22).

The judgment of Jezebel was a bloody sight for all to see. Her body was destroyed, but that same spirit of witchcraft is alive and in operation in many churches today. It is frightening, because we have become so comfortable with manipulation and hype. We have often mistaken it for a move from God. We have lost our spiritual discernment when it comes to this spirit in our midst.

Any attempt to manipulate is witchcraft. When the anointing of God is present, manipulation is not necessary.

Music is for the purpose of worship and worship is to usher in the presence of God, not hype you up to receive a message. It should set the tone for the message, open hearts and minds to hear what the Spirit is saying. In some services it has become like the warm-up act for the main event — lesser known entertainers getting the audience ready for the star.

The star was and forevermore will be the Son of God. He needs little introduction and when He was on this earth He shied away from fanfare. His presence brought the miracles, His words brought healing. His advance publicity didn't change the number of miracles He performed or heighten the anointing of the Word.

COUNT THE COST

One must realize what's at stake when advantage is taken over another. Psalm 112:5 NKJV says, "A good man deals graciously and lends; he will guide his affairs with discretion." Verse 6 goes on to say, "Surely he will never be shaken...." God's people are givers and should never be "takers." Certainly, much of the shaking going on today is the result of manipulating others.

To show mercy to the underprivileged and to extend kindness to those who suffer surely attracts God's attention. Proverbs 19:17 NKJV says, "He who has pity on the poor lends to the Lord, and He will pay back what he has given." The help given to those who are in need becomes God's personal debt. There is no doubt that He will pay His debts!

Often, Jesus would identify religious control over the people. They would impose requirements on others they themselves didn't perform. Child of God, understand that it is His presence that we are talking about. It is His presence we are seeking. You may ask, "You mean to tell me, I risk losing His presence by refusing to show mercy?" The response to that question is an emphatic YES!

UNPROVEN REMARKS

America has become the land where unfounded and unsubstantiated slander is circulated as truth. Unfortunately, the Church has welcomed this same spirit of the world right into the pews of our churches. First Timothy 5:19 NKJV declares, "Do not receive an accusation against an elder except from two or three witnesses."

Please note, those who correct others and preach the Gospel will always have enemies. The accusation must never be believed until it is based on fact, not gossip. Remember, operating in receiving a reward against the innocent will cost you access to God's house.

A powerful principle is seen in Numbers 22:18 NKJV. Balak attempted to hire the prophet Balaam to curse Israel. Note the text: "...Though Balak were to give me his house full of silver and gold, I could not go beyond the word of the Lord my God, to do less or more." The key phrase is to "not go beyond the word of the Lord."

Believers would do well today to stick with what the Word of God has to say about others and reject the opinions of people.

THE GOD OF THE AGE

One great preacher said, "That which is happening in you is greater than that which is happening to you." Second Corinthians 4:1 NKJV states, "Therefore, since we have this ministry, as we have received mercy, we do not lose heart." Recognize the strategy of the devil as he attempts to seduce you into a godless life. To withhold mercy from those who need mercy is Satan's attempt to close the door to God's presence in your life.

The god of this world is no phantom. Even Michael the archangel did not dare to use allusive terms when contending with him (Jude 9). His main arsenal is the art of intimidation. To intimidate is to discourage or restrain from acting by threats of destruction. God's people must *never* walk in this ungodly characteristic.

Second Corinthians 4:4 NKJV declares, "Whose minds the god of this age has blinded...." How many people today have been blinded and have induced blindness on others because of failing to extend mercy?

Second Corinthians 4:2 NKJV records the key to loosing oneself from this awful attitude. First, we are to renounce "the hidden things of shame." That is, completely disown any and all attitudes that cause harm or unnecessary burdens upon others. Next, we are instructed to not walk "in craftiness." Basically, this Scripture is telling us to not "trick" others into something they really don't want to do. Preachers particularly must be very careful to not misrepresent God's Word with a motive to experience self-gain.

Finally, 2 Corinthians 4:2 declares, "...nor handling the word of God deceitfully." The pure in heart are often easily misled when a gifted and charismatic orator convinces them God's Word is asking them to do what is in the heart of the speaker rather than in the heart of God. Satan is content for you and me to know the location of God's house, but he will stop at nothing to prevent our access into God's presence. Too many of God's people have lost their key into God's presence by being caught up in the spirit of manipulation.

ABIDING BRINGS MERCY

I am so thankful that God's mercies are new every morning (Lamentations 3:22,23). Because I have received the mercy of God, I must show mercy in every circumstance I encounter. I may see gross misuse of the things of God, but **He** is big enough to handle it Himself. I am not the judge. I am called to be an intercessor. I am to respond as Aaron and Hur did, holding up the arms of leadership in the most critical battle.

In my passion for the presence of God, I have made a choice to operate in mercy. In abiding with the Father, it is my goal to possess His attributes. He has all power. He could destroy us at any moment, yet with all that power He chooses still to have mercy on His children. How can we do any less?

KEY 5
UNMOVABLE

5

UNMOVABLE

...He that doeth these things shall never be
moved.

Psalm 15:5b

Years ago in the church we used to sing a song
entitled, "I Shall Not Be Moved." Sometimes we joked
about Sister so-and-so not being moved — she never
lifted her arms in praise, clapped her hands, or moved
to her purse when the offering was taken. We knew she
took the words of that song seriously, yet her
actions did not portray the true meaning of the song.

Often, we interpret things to our own advantage.
We are planted in our worship, in our giving, and even
in our spirit man, but our faith continually falters. With
every wind that blows, we question God, blame Him
and cry out in despair.

> But blessed is the man who trusts in the Lord,
> whose confidence is in him.
>
> He will be like a tree planted by the water that
> sends out its roots by the stream.
>
> It does not fear when heat comes; its leaves are
> always green.
>
> It has no worries in a year of drought and never
> fails to bear fruit.
>
> **Jeremiah 17:7,8 NIV**

Jeremiah gave us a precious insight here. This revelation opens the last and most important lock in the process of entering and dwelling in the presence of God.

GET PLANTED

One of the major hindrances to finding this key is the failure on the believer's part to plant himself or herself. We are too busy running to and fro. We tell ourselves we have no time to commit to a local church body. Our social schedules are too busy to be involved in all the Kingdom work.

If you take the time to talk to those who obviously abide in the presence of God, you will find one amazing common denominator in their upbringing — their life **was** the church. Sundays in particular were days of total dedication to God's work. There was a Sunday school class to teach, two services of singing in the choir, a large Sunday dinner where someone was entertained and encouraged in the things of God, a rush to change clothes, then back to church for a special music rehearsal, prayer, then the main service.

When there was a powerful move of the Spirit, you would stay at the altar until all hours of the night — because you were planted. The church was your life, your breath, your heart. You did not want to make it through the week without the Sunday worship experience.

When things went awry in the church, you were planted. It didn't matter what others were saying. When attitudes crossed and purposes were misunderstood, you were planted. When others had struggles and heartaches, you wept with them on the phone and at the altar, because you were planted.

When you had a crisis, the church pulled in around you and supported you through the winds of adversity, because you were planted. The time the pastor resigned and moved away and it seemed the church would never be able to replace him, you were planted.

The new pastor took you through an expensive expansion program, but you were planted. The church voted out your favorite songbook and replaced it with an overhead projector and choruses. It took adjustment, but you were planted. When you are firmly planted in a fellowship where God is the focus, there you will find strength.

When the winds of adversity blow in your personal circumstances, it is critical to be rooted deeply in the things of God. The Great Physician and the Wonderful Counselor is always available when you are abiding in Him.

Children of God experience many of the same heartaches as do people in the world. We live in a godless society where man is given a free will. We are often victims of a sick society with its perversions and valueless standards for human life.

When you as a believer lose a job, a child to drugs or death, a home in a fire or in a cataclysmic weather event, how will you hold up? Are you planted?

Have you ever watched the news reports on TV after a massive storm has leveled an area? You will see debris from homes, overturned vehicles, downed power-lines, and even some uprooted trees. As cameras pan the destruction, I am amazed at some strong trees still standing among the flattened ruins. Those are trees with a strong root system. They simply were not moved when the winds battered them.

The trees may have some branches missing, and leaves and twigs may be missing. Some bark may even be ripped off as debris stripped it while blowing by, but the tree is still standing. Jesus said that it rains on the righteous as well as on the unrighteous (Matthew 5:45). When the rains come, we must be firmly planted in the things of God (Matthew 7:24,25).

Those who are firmly rooted in the things of God are called oaks of righteousness by Isaiah. He goes on to say that we are personal plantings of the Lord for display of His splendor (Isaiah 61:3b). To these oaks of righteousness come some precious promises.

> **They will rebuild the ancient ruins and restore the places long devastated; they will renew the ruined cities that have been devastated for generations.**

> **Aliens will shepherd your flocks; foreigners will work your fields and vineyards.**

> **And you will be called priests of the Lord, you will be named ministers of our God.**

> **You will feed on the wealth of nations, and in their riches you will boast.**

> **Instead of their shame my people will receive a double portion, and instead of disgrace they will rejoice in their inheritance; and so they will inherit a double portion in their land, and everlasting joy will be theirs.**

> **Isaiah 61:4-7 NIV**

What precious promises await those planted by the Lord. Those who abide in His presence will receive a double portion of the wealth of nations, their lands, plus everlasting joy. Now that makes me want to be planted more than ever.

I want to see devastated places restored in the lives of those around me. Families who have lived in devastation for generations I will see renewed as I abide in the presence of God. We must have a renewal of the spirit that says, "It doesn't matter how bad the storm, God is greater."

Just as I see those sturdy trees standing after a storm, Isaiah records, "All who see them will acknowledge that they are a people the Lord has blessed" (Isaiah 61:9b NIV). God will showcase us. We will stand tall above the mess of mankind, if we have been planted — if we are truly a planting of the Lord.

We must be like the wise man Jesus referred to in Matthew 7. He built his house on the rock. His dwelling place was rooted in the firm foundation of the things of God.

> The rain came down, the streams rose, and the winds blew and beat against that house; yet it did not fall, because it had its foundation on the rock.
>
> **Matthew 7:25 NIV**

I Shall Not Be Moved

You can decide not to be moved. You can make a positive statement of faith that nothing will move you. You can write it, speak it and put it on your letterhead, but if you are not planted, you will be uprooted at the first breeze. To be planted requires a quality decision. If you are rooted in God, it will show. You will stand as an example to others when trials attempt to take you out.

People will look at your life and marvel. How is it that you did not lose faith when your diagnosis was cancer? They will wonder how you stayed so positive and landed another job so quickly. What made such a difference for you when your daughter experienced such deep rebellion and scarred her life? How did you forgive and go on?

Your ability to stand in the midst of life's storms will be a testimony not only to those in the world but to those in the Body of Christ, seeking to know God more — longing to go deeper in Him. You will be their example, their Farmers' Almanac for complete planting instructions.

> **Therefore, my dear brothers, stand firm. Let nothing move you. Always give yourselves fully to the work of the Lord, because you know that your labor in the Lord is not in vain.**
>
> **1 Corinthians 15:58** NIV

HEALTHY ROOT SYSTEM

Jeremiah knew the importance of the **living water**. He had planted his roots by a stream. God had spoken to Jeremiah to write down all the predictions given to him. When the prophecies were actually read in the temple, the leadership wouldn't listen to the full message. After hearing only a few pages, they were so enraged that they cut the scroll in pieces and threw it into a fire.

I can just imagine according to human nature what Jeremiah must have felt at this point. "Why God, didn't You tell me to write it? Isn't it Your Word? Aren't You supposed to watch over Your Word to perform it?

Where are You, God? Are You listening? Oh God, You are not hearing me. I know You have forgotten me."

The Scripture does not record what Jeremiah thought. It does, however, record what he said and did. He spoke to his scribe and simply said, "Take another scroll and write on it [again]" (Jeremiah 36:28 NIV).

WRITE IT AGAIN

When you have your root system feeding from the streams of living water, when you have been abiding in the presence of God, you will have all that you need to write it again.

You may have lost your marriage through some diabolical attack of Satan. Perhaps the enemy of your soul is telling you that you can no longer be a priest or a minister unto God or have a word for the people. I say, write it again!

Your ministry may have experienced a devastating blow financially, or criticism has come to wound you. I say, stand up tall. Do not be tossed by winds of adversity. You may have lost a little bark. You may be feeling scraped and bruised. You may have lost some leaves and even some weak branches have blown away, but take another scroll and write it again.

Perhaps your children have taken a path that is far from what you taught them. They may be suffering the sting of sin and paying a huge price for their mistakes. Don't give up. Do not beat yourself over the head. Stop looking for all the ways you failed, and stop taking the blame. If there are things God has issue with in your life, He will deal with you in His presence. Don't be downcast or downhearted. Remember God's promises, and take another scroll and write it again.

It would not have done any good for Jeremiah to moan and groan. He didn't waste time with "should have," "could have," "would have" woes. What was done was done. He knew what God had told him to do, and even though it was a setback, he decided just to do it again.

JUST DO IT — AGAIN!

Too often we simply give up, give in, or give out when circumstances impede our progress in the things of the Spirit. We want to give up on ourselves and on God. If someone else has failed us or wounded us, we get mad at God. "How could He let this happen to me?" we wonder. It is the natural tendency of man to question, "Why?" However, when we take the time to do that, it throws us off course. It causes a delay in our journey of faith. Yes, there are those who have done us wrong. But we must remember that God anticipated it, and He saw it, not as a hindrance to what He had planned for us, so why should we see it as a hindrance?

When someone has failed us, wronged us, or wounded us, we must learn to be unmovable. We can stop for only a moment on our quest for His presence. It may be important to our spiritual growth to evaluate for a moment our role in the matter, to look inside for a brief attitude check. You might inquire of God as to your role in the matter — where or if you failed. To a heart that truly longs for His presence, God will speak swiftly, with compassion and love. Just know for sure, Satan will attempt anything in order to remove you from God's presence.

SHAKE IT OFF

> And when Paul had gathered a bundle of sticks, and laid them on the fire, there came a viper out of the heat, and fastened on his hand.
>
> And when the barbarians saw the venomous beast hang on his hand, they said among themselves, No doubt this man is a murderer, whom, though he hath escaped the sea, yet vengeance suffereth not to live.
>
> And he shook off the beast into the fire, and felt no harm.
>
> Acts 28:3-5

This story in Paul's missionary journey contains some important lessons for us today. He had just arrived on the island of Melita about seventy-five miles south of Sicily. He had just gone through a life-threatening storm on the sea.

When the ship on which he had been traveling ran aground, the front part of the vessel remained wedged, but the back part of the ship broke up as the waves crashed against it. He had arrived on the island only because he had grabbed on to one of the broken pieces from the ship, and it brought him safely into the harbor. (This was in response to God Who said, "Stay with the ship.")

Paul's passion for God had already been tested, or so it would seem. He arrived wet, weary and riding on a broken piece of what he felt was his safe ministry vehicle (Acts 27:41-44). He salvaged some dry wood to make a fire to warm himself after his cold, terrifying journey. Your "ship" may not be intact at this moment, but just hold on to whatever piece you can find!

The very ones he had come to minister to were watching him curiously and closely. When Paul lit the wood, a poisonous snake from the woodpile decided to get out of the heat. It lurched from the fire and bit Paul's hand.

As the heathen island people looked on, they judged Paul to be a murderer who, after surviving the shipwreck, was now going to receive his full sentence.

Scripture does not record Paul's attitude or even his words at this moment, just one divine action that we must not take for granted. He **shook off** the attacker. Before he ever brought a word of Gospel to the people of the island, his actions ministered loudly.

The people watched in amazement as *no poison took hold of Paul's system.* As they continued to watch, they decided that he was not a murderer as they had suspected, but a god. Because of his testimony, the entire island would listen and receive. He was able to minister there three months, and many were healed.

When we are stung by some poisonous bite, we don't react as well. Usually we complain for a while about the pain. We make a dozen calls to loved ones to tell them about our hurt and ask their opinion on what to do. We want someone to sympathize over our pain. We want our friends and family to hate the viper that bit us. A big bandage is in order so everyone will ask us what happened and we can tell it again and again. *SHAKE IT OFF!*

Paul's passion for the presence of God made him immune to Satan's attempts to thwart his ministry. He knew what he was called to do. He burned with passion for the things of God. He knew the power of

God that was available for the taking when trials, troubles and heartaches came.

He did not let one little shipwreck followed by one poisonous snake bite stop him. He had arrived on broken pieces. Surely he could survive a venomous attack.

It is not popular in this day of psychology just to "shake off" bitter words or bitter circumstances. We are counseled, coddled and carried through our difficult times with a million self-help books and TV talk shows that sing the same sad "Somebody's Done Me Wrong" song. We watch others who have been hurt and don't feel so alone. We nurse our unforgiveness and our grudges until it would almost take a lightning bolt from heaven to take our attention off of our pity party.

It is time for the Church to live what it teaches — to practice what it preaches — shake it off. We don't have enough time to dwell on junk. The call of God does not allow for delay. We must be about the Father's business.

Unmovable, steady, unshaken. These are the qualities we must exhibit as a result of our passion for His presence. His dwelling place, His abode is our destination and anything that would seek to deter us, we possess the power to overcome.

Whatever has sought to hold you back, shake it off. Forgive the pain of the past and those who have inflicted it. No longer dwell on the serpent, but get your eyes back on the prize. Jesus said that for the joy of the prize that was set before Him, He could even endure the pain of the cross (Hebrews 12:2). It was but a moment in time that insured life for eternity.

Shake off your moment in time. That devastating event or harsh circumstance that has kept you from going on with God. This is your moment to take hold of the **Unmovable key** and to press on toward the mark of the prize of the high calling of God in Christ Jesus (Philippians 3:14). Now, put the key in the lock, open the door and enter into His presence.

PUT YOUR HANDS ABOVE YOUR HEAD AND DON'T MOVE

Whenever you watch an old western movie, this is a line you will hear often: "Put your hands above your head and don't move." The bad guys borrowed a spiritual principle right out of heaven! Satan knew the sign of surrender and the focus that was placed on the One Who was the object of the worship.

Surrender means "to relinquish possession or control of to another as a result of demand or compulsion."[9] When the bad guys yell, "Get your hands in the air," they are making a demand. When we raise our hands in surrender to God, we should be doing so from divine compulsion. That is, the Spirit is compelling us to surrender fully to the divine will of God.

Too often we must be encouraged to lift our hands, or we are told to do so from the platform. We are rarely ready to relinquish full control to God, our heavenly Father. I have heard every excuse in the book for someone not wanting to raise their hands. Some say they are shy, while others say that they are uncomfortable with a display of emotion. The best excuse I ever heard was one man who insisted he had body odor and didn't want to advertise it to his neighbor. I say, "Get some deodorant, brother, and begin to surrender the rest of your stinking self to God!"

By lifting our hands in surrender to God, we are saying, "God, I am taking my hands off the situations in my life. I am giving up all that I have done and all that I have been trying to do to You." It is time to give up.

WHAT DO YOU HAVE IN YOUR HANDS?

What have you been holding on to? What has been weighing you down? Aren't you tired of carrying such a heavy load? How long before you turn it over to Jesus? How about right now? Don't wait until the next church service to surrender to God. Get your hands in the air right now where you are sitting and surrender your life completely to Him.

Surrender the hurts of the past, your bitterness toward others for their wrongs, your unforgiveness, your habits and hobbies that are not of God. It is time to give up. Give up and get out of that rut. You desire a daily experience of the presence of God, but you have been afraid to surrender your all.

I don't need to tell you what you need to surrender. The Holy Spirit will reveal it to you as you ask Him. Most people know all too well what has been standing between them and God.

DON'T MOVE

Once you have surrendered your all to Him, don't move. "Those who trust in the Lord are like Mount Zion, which cannot be shaken but endures forever" (Psalm 125:1 NIV). Stay in an attitude of surrender and worship, and allow God to place in your hand the last key to His presence. You don't want to move because you do not want to miss one single word He longs to share with you. Where do you have to go anyway? You never again want to be out of His presence. You have surrendered all your ability and your plans to Him, now let Him work for a change. When He is ready for you to move, He will give you direction.

You will come to hear His voice more clearly because you have removed all hindrances. The world can no longer drown out His Word because you are in His presence. You will no more find your fulfillment in the things of this world, because you now have a passion only for the presence of God.

You have been given the keys. Now, decide to enter in, and you will find a peace and contentment you have never known. You will be amazed at the spiritual things that will be birthed in you as a result of your intimate relationship with the Lord.

CONCLUSION

REMEMBER THESE KEYS:

Key 1 — Be CAREFUL of your neighbor.

Key 2 — Be WATCHFUL of your company.

Key 3 — Be FAITHFUL to God's Word and to your own words.

Key 4 — Be MERCIFUL toward others.

Key 5 — Be UNMOVABLE in your faith.

It is my desire that your passion for God will cause you to use these keys today, and open the door to the precious presence of God.

Endnotes

[1]*Webster's, II New Riverside University Dictionary*, copyright 1984, Boston MA, p. 448.

[2]*Merriam-Webster's Collegiate Dictionary*, Tenth Ed. (Springfield, MA: Merriam-Webster, Inc.), 1996, p. 1317.

[3]William Barclay. *The Letter to the Romans*, Revised Ed., The Daily Bible Study Series. (Philadelphia, PA: The Westminister Press), 1975, p. 33.

[4]*Webster's, II New Riverside University Dictionary*, copyright 1984, Boston MA, p. 998.

[5]Dake, Finis Jennings. *Dake's Annotated Reference Bible.* (Lawrenceville, GA: Dake Bible Sales, Inc.), 1961, 1989, New Testament p. 161.

[6]James Patterson. *The Day America Told the Truth.* (Prentice Hall Plublishing, New York, NY) copyright 1991, pg. 142-143

[7]William Backus. *Learning To Tell Myself the Truth*, A Six-Week Guide To Freedom From Anger, Anxiety, Depression and Perfectionism. (Minneapolis, MN: Bethany House Publishers), 1994, p. 32.

[8] *Merriam-Webster's Collegiate Dictionary*, Op. Cit., p. 1302.

[9]*Webster's, II New Riverside University Dictionary*, copyright 1984, Boston MA, p. 1166.

About the Author

Louis F. Kayatin is a man of compassion for the lost and needy souls of the world. For over twenty-two years he has served as the Senior Pastor of Church on the North Coast in Lorain, Ohio, ministering God's Word with authority and power. Louis is a gifted communicator, having an anointed style that allows him to preach and teach the Scriptures with acute clarity. The message he delivers is restoring the end-time dynamics of the Pentecostal message. Under the anointing of the Holy Spirit, Pastor Kayatin releases a refreshing and a renewing touch of God to his world-wide audiences.

Louis Kayatin was saved at the age of twenty-three in the city of Lorain, Ohio. His unique testimony includes a former life of involvement with a neighborhood gang. God's divine destiny for Louis Kayatin not only allowed him to be saved at the church he now pastors, but also to evangelize the city of Lorain in which he was raised!

Church on the North Coast is a flourishing and all-encompassing ministry whose goal is to establish an undeniable testimony of the lordship of Jesus Christ in Northeastern Ohio and throughout the world. Today, in addition to his duties as Senior Pastor of Church on the North Coast, he ministers across the globe in such countries as Nigeria, England and Russia. He assisted in the coordination of the "Feed the Hungry" Program with Dr. Lester Sumrall in Nicaragua where thousands were fed daily.

Church on the North Coast's media outreach, *Wall of Fire*, consists of a daily radio and television program. *Wall of Fire* television is viewed by thousands in the Northern Ohio area. The radio broadcast is heard in Ohio, Indiana and Illinois. He previously authored, *Understanding Seed: The Real Truth About the Harvest*.

Louis Kayatin is married, and his wife, Tina, co-pastors with him. They have three daughters, one son and three grandchildren.

Product
Teaching materials by Louis F. Kayatin

Tape Series

The Family	10 tapes	45.00*
Words	8 tapes	40.00*
Agreement	8 tapes	40.00*
The Religious Spirit	7 tapes	32.00*
Faithfulness is a Force	6 tapes	28.00*
Fear	5 tapes	26.00*
Blessings and Curses	4 tapes	22.00*
The Gates of Faith	3 tapes	14.00*
Building you House	3 tapes	14.00*
Love and Humility	2 tapes	10.00*
Releasing the Holy Spirit	2 tapes	10.00*
Trouble your Trouble	2 tapes	10.00*
The Dangers of Despondency	2 tapes	10.00*
The Gifts of Faith	2 tapes	10.00*
The Gift of Miracles	2 tapes	10.00*
The Gift of Healing	2 tapes	10.00*
Loyalty	2 tapes	10.00*
Responsibility	2 tapes	10.00*

Bold print denotes most recent series

Marriage Tapes

Keys to A Successful Marriage	7.00*
How to Affair Proof Your Marriage	7.00*
Talk To Me	7.00*

CLASSIC TAPE SINGLES

Tapes $7.00 each*

The Lamb's Wife
Great Grace
Why the delay when I pray
Defeat Depression
Confidence is not Cosmetic
Responding To Anger
Top Down, Bottom Up
Axing Anxiety

Going Beyond Your Beyond
Nature of Lust and how
    to Defeat It
The Sun Is Very Hot
The Sound of Rain
The Labels People Wear
Time to Turn North
Pressing in

CNC MUSIC

	CD	Cassette
Standing Strong	15.00*	10.00*
Alone with God	15.00*	10.00*
Campmeeting Live	15.00*	10.00*

MINISTRY INFORMATION

CNC Annual Campmeeting — 2nd week of August
Local Church Seminar — call for information

Louis F. Kayatin is a sought-after Conference and Campmeeting speaker. For ministry availability, please contact (216) 960-1100

Visit Church on the North Coast at our Web Site:
www.cncchurch.org

We accept MasterCard, Visa, American Express

* All prices include shipping and handling costs

Church on the North Coast
4125 Leavitt Road (Rt. 58) • Lorain, OH 44053
(216) 960-1100